LET'S VISIT FIJI

Let's visit
FIJI

JOHN BALL AND CHRIS FAIRCLOUGH

DEDICATION

Dedicated to Debbie, Joey, Ben and Tyron
—my family and my inspiration.

ACKNOWLEDGEMENTS

The author and photographer wish to thank the Fiji Visitors Bureau in Suva, The Fijian Consulate and the Fijian Visitors Bureau in Auckland, and all the people too numerous to mention who gave freely of their time and hospitality, and who shared with us a little of what is special about Fiji and Fijians. Without your help and inspiration this book would not have been possible.

The illustration of Captain James Cook is reproduced by permission of The Australian Information Service, London.

CIP data

Ball, John, 1949 –
   Let's visit Fiji.
   1. Fiji – Social life and customs – Juvenile literature
   I. Title   II. Fairclough, Chris
   996'.11   DU600

ISBN 0 222 00984 5

Burke Publishing Company Limited
Pegasus House, 116-120 Golden Lane, London EC1Y 0TL, England.
Burke Publishing (Canada) Limited
Registered Office: 20 Queen Street West, Suite 3000, Box 30, Toronto, Canada M5H 1V5.
Burke Publishing Company Inc.
Registered Office: 333 State Street, PO Box 1740, Bridgeport, Connecticut 06601, U.S.A.
Filmset in Baskerville by Graphiti (Hull) Ltd., Hull, England.
Colour reproduction by Swift Graphics (UK) Ltd., Southampton, England.
Printed in Singapore by Tien Wah Press (Pte.) Ltd.

". . . . for one of the rare jewels of the world is the genuine Fijian smile. It starts slowly, it illuminates the whole face, it rests there long enough to be clearly recognized and recognize clearly, and it fades with secret slowness as it passes by."

Eric Berne, M.D.

Contents

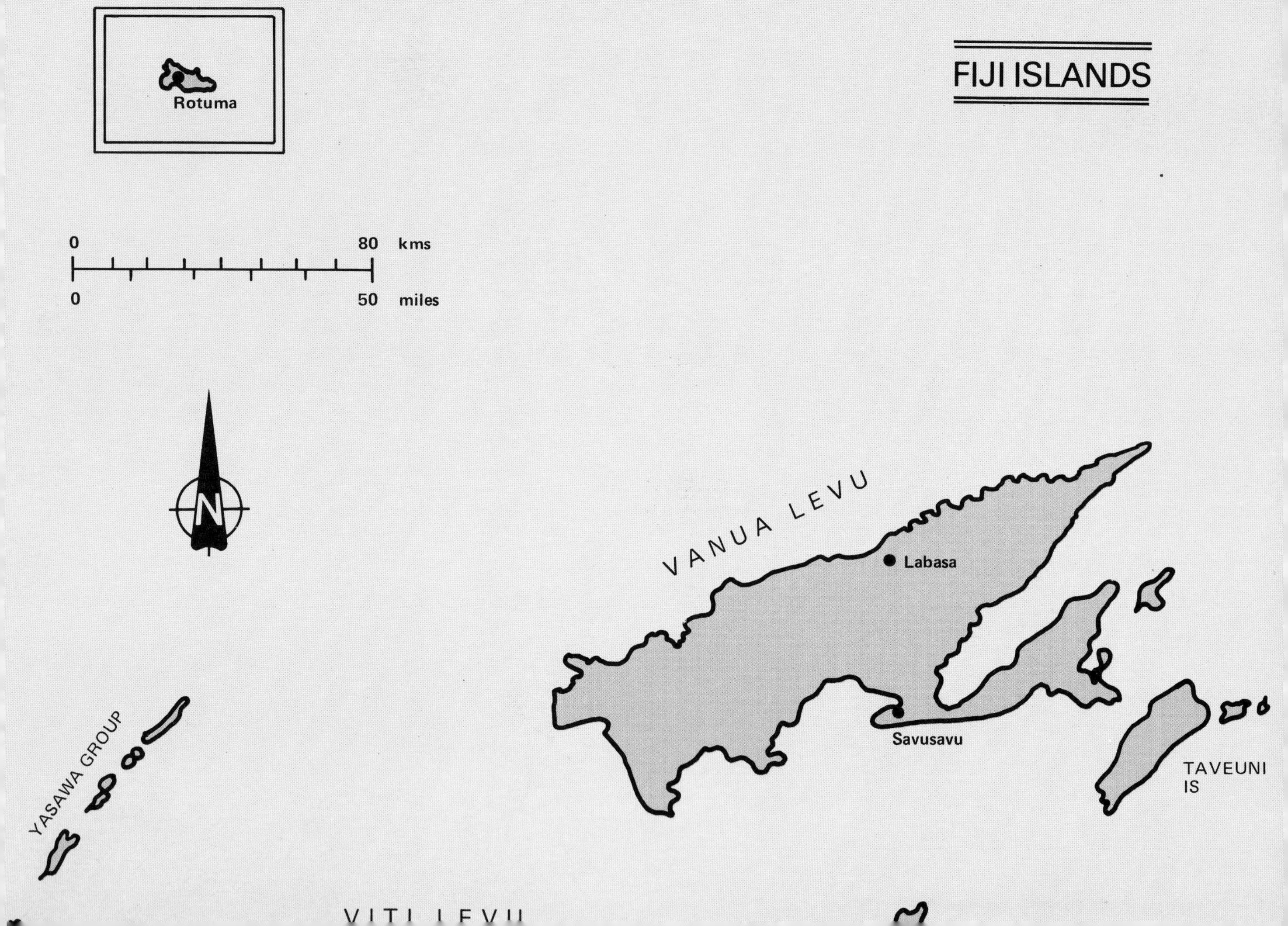

FIJI ISLANDS

Rotuma

80 kms

50 miles

N

VANUA LEVU

● Labasa

Savusavu

TAVEUNI
IS

VITI LEVU

YASAWA GROUP

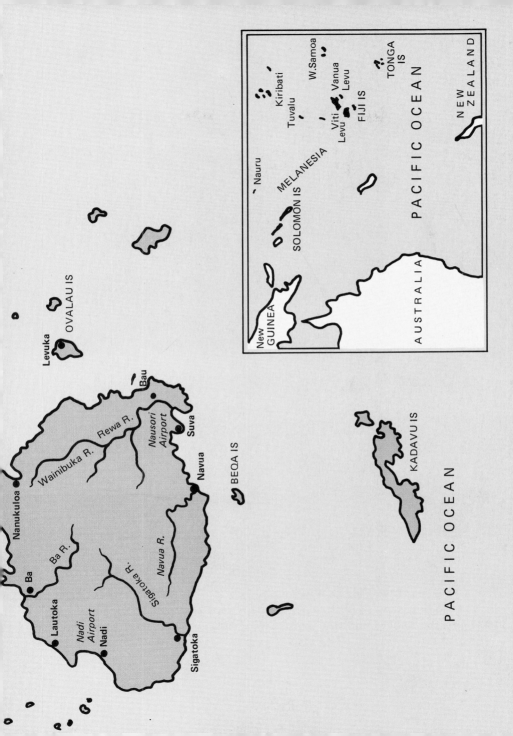

OVALAU IS

Levuka

Nanukuloa

Ba

Lautoka

Nadi
Nadi Airport

Sigatoka

Sigatoka R.

Navua R.

Navua

Suva

Nausori Airport

Bau

Rewa R.

Wainibuka R.

Ba R.

BEQA IS

KADAVU IS

PACIFIC OCEAN

New GUINEA

Nauru

SOLOMON IS

MELANESIA

Kiribati

Tuvalu

W.Samoa

Vanua Levu

Viti Levu

FIJI IS

TONGA IS

NEW ZEALAND

PACIFIC OCEAN

AUSTRALIA

One of the tiny islands which make up this ''tropical paradise'' located between the Pacific and the Caribbean

A Dot in the Ocean

Spin your world globe and look for Fiji. After some searching you will see a dot in the Pacific—just to the east of Australia. That's Fiji.

Fiji is actually about 332 dots, or islands, spread over 116,000 square kilometres (45,000 square miles) of ocean. About one hundred of these are inhabited. Only two are large. Among these islands live people from Micronesia and Melanesia (island groups in the West Pacific), India and Polynesia (the island group which includes New Zealand, Hawaii and Samoa). Radio stations broadcast in English, Fijian and Hindustani. There are no passenger trains and there is no television.

Fiji has some villages which have changed little in three thousand years. Alongside them are luxury hotels offering the latest in western culture. Fiji is a small nation forging a place in the modern world. It is also a tropical paradise. The Fijians are a people with much to teach the world. A people who have mastered the art of enjoying life. This makes Fiji an exciting place.

Before exploring Fiji, it would be helpful to learn how to pronounce some Fijian words and names. Originally, Fijians had no written language. When the first Europeans arrived in Fiji, they wrote out the language, using English letters. Some

9

sounds were difficult to copy into English sounds, so they used a shortening, which is now the standard way of writing Fijian.

All Fijian names in this book are written using this standard. Take a few minutes now to learn the basics:

b is pronounced *mb* as in nu*mb*er
c is pronounced *th* as in *th*is
d is pronounced *nd* as in sa*nd*
g is pronounced *ng* as in si*ng*
q is pronounced *ngg* as in fi*ng*er

Here are some words used in the book, and next to them is their phonetic pronunciation:

*B*ula is pronounced *mb*ula
Na*d*i is pronounced Na*nd*i
Ka*d*avu is pronounced Ka*nd*avu
*C*ako*b*au is pronounced *Th*ako*mb*au
Ya*q*ona is pronounced Ya*ngg*ona
Ta*g*imau*c*ia is pronounced Ta*ng*imau*th*ia
*Beq*a is pronounced *Mb*e*ngg*a
Lutunasa*b*oso*b*a is pronounced Lutunaso*mb*aso*mb*a
Si*g*atoka is pronounced Si*ng*atoka
Dakuwa*q*u is pronounced Dakuwa*ngg*u

It is only *b, c, d, g* and *q,* that change. Other words and names are pronounced as they are written, for example: Drua, Masi,

A typical village on one of Fiji's one hundred inhabited islands

Isa Lei, Vanua, tanoa, Lovo, Yasawa, Levuka, Lautoka, Levu.

One last thing: the emphasis is generally on the penultimate (second to last) syllable *e.g.* matagali is pronounced *ma-ta-GA-li*.

Now let's discover these exciting islands, and understand the lure they hold for people of all cultures.

11

Sunshine, Hurricanes and Volcanoes

When learning about another country, a good starting-point is its weather. This is possibly the greatest single influence on the way people live, on local plants and animals and even on the shape of the land itself.

Fiji is no exception to this. Being in the tropics, between 15 degrees and 22 degrees south of the equator, means there is much sunshine, but much heavy rainfall too. Visitors often find it hard to believe when they visit Fiji in June, July and August, and spend their time sun-bathing and swimming, that this is the middle of the Fijian winter! Summer in Fiji is the wet season. In Suva (the capital), that brings an average rainfall of over 3,000 millimetres (120 inches). Not quite as wet, though, as Taveuni—one of the off-shore islands—which suffers nearly 5,800 millimetres (228 inches)!

Being a group of islands in a large ocean, Fiji has what is known as a Tropical Maritime climate. This means that it never gets too hot or too cold. Temperatures stay mostly between 20 and 30 degrees Celsius (68 and 86 degrees Fahrenheit). This can be contrasted with Central Australia, which is about the same distance south of the equator but in the middle of a continent, so that it gets very hot—40 degrees Celsius (104 degrees Fahrenheit)—then drops to freezing-point at night. And

Palm-shaded beaches like this are just one of the attractions for visitors to Fiji, many of whom wish to sun-bathe and swim

in Central Australia it hardly ever rains; the land here is a desert. By contrast, Fiji has much lush tropical growth.

But, once in a while, nature frowns on Fiji, as if to make sure that this ideal climate is not taken for granted. The Fijians believe that the first warning has been given once sea-birds start flying inland. Talk of hurricanes spreads rapidly. Then people stock up with essentials such as food, candles and hurricane-lamps.

This usually occurs between October and March. Fiji lies in an area often ravaged by hurricanes, with winds that can reach a force of 180 kilometres (over 111 miles) per hour. Though Fiji has an efficient alert system, no one can predict exactly where the eye of the hurricane will pass.

In 1972, a hurricane (code-named Bebe) struck the islands with a rare intensity. Total villages were wiped out, people were killed, and crops destroyed. The winds reached an amazing 190 kilometres (118 miles) per hour. It was estimated that 50,000 Fijians were left homeless. The next day, as if it had never happened, the sun was shining. Surrounded by total destruction, the Fijians began to clean up. The surrounding Pacific countries were quick to respond to the disaster. Emergency food, medical aid and materials were flown in. Villages were rebuilt and new crops planted. Fijians can but hope that a long time will pass before anything of such force strikes again.

There is yet another factor which affects the weather in Fiji. The islands lie in the path of the trade winds which blow from east to south-east all year round. Because of Fiji's geography

14

these winds have varying effects. The main islands—Viti Levu and Vanua Levu—have high volcanic mountains, with towns and cities dotted around the coastline. These mountains form a barrier against the trade winds that bring the rain-bearing clouds. The clouds often burst against the mountains, giving a lot more rain on the eastern (or windward) side of the island. The city of Suva, for example, on the eastern side of Viti Levu is renowned for its heavy rainfall. There are days when the atmosphere is very hot and sticky, and at the same time rain is pouring down! Lautoka, which is opposite on the western side of Viti Levu, is fortunate not to suffer from such humid weather, as the mountains disperse the clouds before they reach it.

All around the coast, daytime sea breezes bring relief from

Volcanic mountains, typical of Viti Levu and Vanua Levu

A policeman on duty in Lautoka, on the western side of Viti Levu—
protected by the mountains from the rain-clouds which often burst
over Suva

the heat and humidity. But up in the highlands, away from these breezes, there is high humidity. These are ideal conditions for the dense rain forest which covers the mountains. Quite a variety for such a small area: lovely clear warm days, hot sticky humidity, hurricanes and rain forests.

Fiji's geography is also full of variety. The main islands are volcanic. They were formed millions of years ago by movements between the continental plates—the name given to the huge pieces which form the earth's crust. This caused parts to buckle upwards. Volcanic eruptions from the fractures caused, formed steep rocky-sided mountains. Slowly, erosion wore down parts of the surface to make fertile plains. The ocean waves formed white sandy beaches.

These volcanic islands contrast strongly with the coral atolls. Starting on a rock foundation near the surface of the sea, layer upon layer of fragile coral polyps grow. These are jelly-like animals (looking like small plants). They form a hard skeletal shell of carbonate of lime. If the conditions are favourable, countless thousands establish themselves in colonies. The mass builds up over centuries to form a solid limestone reef.

The polyp has a very simple structure. The mouth in the centre of the coral shell is surrounded by tentacles. These are extended, like threads, for feeding. Polyps generally feed only at night when the minute zoo-plankton organisms (which they live on) rise to the surface.

The coral reef is created largely by the action of polyps. It also consists of many other types of coral, living and dead, and

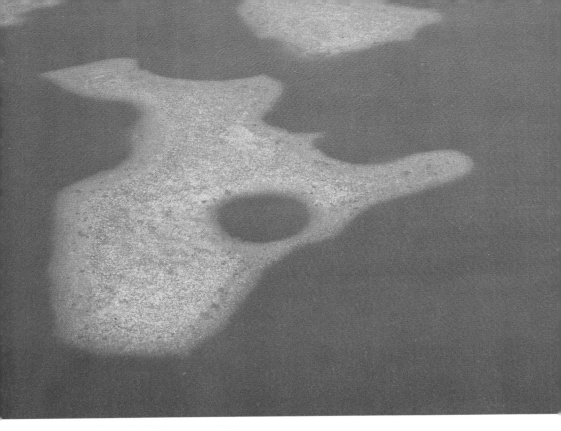

A coral reef with a central lagoon

of sand, mud and clay, which is washed into the coral. All this is cemented together by the continuous wave action. The reef tends to grow outwards in a large circle or ring, forming a lagoon on the inside. Storm waves may break boulders from the reef, and pile them up above the surface level. Vegetation soon becomes established, and an atoll, or coral cay is formed. Islands formed in this way are generally not very high, but they are protected from the ocean waves by the reef which grows around them. During a storm the ocean rollers break on the reef, out to sea. By comparison, the water in the lagoon seems calm.

These sheltered lagoons are a garden of colourful plants and fish. They are a delight for tourists to explore, and they provide a nutritious food source for the Fijians.

Fiji's large islands are volcanic. The very small ones are coral cays. Some islands are a combination of the two. The island of Beqa, for example, is a volcano which erupted in the centre of a coral lagoon! And most volcanic islands have coral reefs growing around their coastlines.

Lizards, Turtles and Rare Flowers

Most of the animals in Fiji were introduced from other countries. They include domestic animals, such as pigs and dogs, introduced by the Fijians long before the Europeans arrived. Horses and cows, goats and cats were brought over by the early Europeans. So were four other animals now considered pests. The first of these is the giant toad. This was introduced from Hawaii in 1936. It was hoped that it would control slugs, beetles and millipedes. It did so, but also increased enormously in numbers. When the toads ran out of insects they started eating each other. The species also became smaller in size. These days, after the rain, the toads come out by the thousands, squatting on lawns and roads.

The second of these animals is the mongoose. Brought over from India, it was introduced to control the hordes of rats which caused great damage to the sugar-cane plantations. The mongoose did this very well but it multiplied quickly under the ideal conditions, and is now a threat to poultry and native birdlife. Though Fiji has tried many different ways of controlling the mongoose, these animals still abound.

The other species which are considered pests, are the mynah and bulbul birds. In populated areas they have aggressively chased the smaller native birds inland. These two birds are squabbling, noisy nuisances, especially the mynah, which has some unattractive habits, such as flying through open windows and doors seaching for food. It also gathers all sorts of rubbish to build its nest in the eaves of houses.

Fiji's indigenous animals—those native to the islands—are few in numbers, but quite varied. There is the native (or Polynesian) rat, now controlled by the mongoose but once, long ago, part of the Fijian's diet. Then there is the flying fox—a black sightless bat—which finds its way to food by using its sense of smell. These creatures have a small fox-like head, and a wing-span of over thirty centimetres (nearly twelve inches). In some areas they can be seen in their hundreds, screeching and clawing in the trees at sunset.

Fiji and Tonga are both the home of the banded iguana—a large and spectacular tree-dwelling lizard. No one has been able to explain how this creature, which is very similar to a South American lizard, managed to migrate so far from any major land-masses. Two-thirds of the iguana's total length consists of a thin twig-like tail. A rich emerald green with bands of brown or blue-grey, the male is a spectacular sight. The female has similar green colouring, but does not have the cross bands. An exciting feature of iguanas is their ability to change colour, and to control their body temperature. In direct sunlight, their skin colour darkens, enabling the cold-blooded reptile to absorb the heat. When the iguana gets too hot, the colour suddenly fades, and his body cools down. A very efficient thermostat!

A sea-cucumber. These harmless creatures which live in the ocean are often found on the shore

Fiji is said to be free of snakes, but on islands where there are no mongooses, harmless varieties of snake do exist. In the ocean, however, there is the black-and-white banded sea-snake which possesses a venom as deadly as that of an Indian cobra. Although not a common sight, these sea-snakes are sometimes found in shallow waters. Despite their dangerous venom, there are no records of anyone having been killed by one.

22

Fiji also has about eighty species of native birds. Mostly small and shy, they are generally found in the highlands and forest areas. Among the more spectacular is the kula, a parrot with deep maroon-coloured feathers. The kula was almost hunted to extinction because its feathers were used to adorn the garments of chiefs.

The gaily-coloured kaka parrot is well-known for its ability to talk by copying words and sounds. There are also many beautiful varieties of fantails, owls and thrushes. In the coastal waters, there are wading birds, such as the heron, and migratory sea-birds.

But if there is one thing in Fiji which overawes every visitor it is the marine life. Divers claim that Fiji is one of the world's top five diving-spots. And it is easy to see why. Fiji has the world's second largest coral reef formation, and this means an abundance of fish and other marine life. Add to this underwater visibility of up to 65 metres (213 feet) and you can well imagine how spectacular it is. Even along the main island coastline, visibility stretches to 30 metres (98 feet).

Most visitors are first introduced to Fiji's underwater world with a snorkel and face mask on the coral reefs. Floating in shallow warm waters, they are in for an awesome experience. Every imaginable colour—yellow, purple, dazzling electric blues, emerald green and stripes galore—schools of tiny fish brush past. They seem oblivious to any intrusion.

There is very little need to move around or look any further. The diver can stay mesmorized in the same place, watching this exciting marine world pass by. The parade is endless, including spotted puffer-fish, dainty golden damsels, the black and white moorish idol-fish and the quaint little box-fish. Add to this a backdrop of coral gardens—branchlets tipped with pink, lavender and blue, and fine coral fans—and you can see how Fiji gained its reputation.

Travelling out across the reef, the visitors leave the warm shallow waters, and suddenly reach the breathtaking "drop offs". Imagine floating in warm water and looking over the edge of the reef to the 200-metre (656-foot) depths. Many a novice has decided to turn back at this point! These waters are the home of many species of Fiji's larger fish. Schools of huge caranx (a mackerel-like fish) and barracuda, sharks and even whales cruise these depths around the reefs. Today, these waters are enjoyed by sports fishermen, but for centuries Fijians have relied on this natural food source.

The Fijians are very skilled fishermen. They have a variety of methods, new and old, for catching their fish. A now-famous method is the *yarayara,* or fish drive. Used mostly when huge quantities of food are required for a village feast (on the occasion of a marriage or death perhaps), the fish drive often requires the participation of the entire village. It is a very exciting adventure, carried out in the shallower areas of the reefs. The villagers take a long, strong vine, with leaves attached, out to the water in little boats. They form this vine into a large circle, with each of the villagers holding onto the vine and beating the sea-bed with wooden poles. This scares the fish into staying

24

A scene in the fishmarket at Labasa. Fijians have always relied on fish as a food source

within the circle, which is gradually made smaller. An exit is then made with a net stretched across it. The fish rush towards the opening and are caught in the net.

A more leisurely method is wading out to waist-deep waters, and catching fish with bait held in a basket made out of dried

25

A Taveuni boy with his catch

coconut leaves. The Fijians will stand for hours on end, hauling in ten to twenty medium-sized fish, plenty for a satisfying dinner!

Turtles are also abundant. They form an important part in Fiji's diet and customs. Turtle steaks cooked in coconut cream are one of the Fijians' favourite dishes. There are many legends

26

A turtle—important in both legend and diet in Fiji

about the turtle. One of the best-known comes from the island of Kadavu:

> The village of Namuana nestles at the foot of a
> charming bay in Vunisea Harbour. Long, long ago
> a beautiful princess called Tinaicoboga lived here. She
> was the wife of the Chief of Namuana Village.
> Tinaicoboga had a charming daughter called
> Raudalice, and the two women often went fishing on
> the reefs around their home.
>
> On one particular occasion, Tinaicoboga and

Raudalice went further afield than usual. They waded out onto the submerged reefs which jut out from the rocky headland to the east of the bay.

They became so engrossed with their fishing that they did not notice the stealthy approach of a great war-canoe, filled with warriors from the nearby village of Nabukelevu.

Suddenly, the warriors leapt from their canoe and seized the two women. They bound their hands and feet with vines, tossed them into the bottom of their canoe, and set off for home with great speed. Although the women pleaded for their lives, the cruel warriors from Nabukelevu were deaf to their pleadings, and would not listen.

The Gods of the Sea, however, were kind and soon a great storm arose. The canoe was tossed about by great waves, and began to fill with water. As the canoe was floundering, the warriors were astounded to notice that the two women had suddenly changed into turtles. To save their own lives, the men seized them and threw them into the sea.

As they swam away the weather changed, and there were no more waves. The warriors returned to their home village, and the women, who had been changed into turtles, lived in the water of the bay.

Ever since then, the maidens of Namuana have sung a special song to their lost princesses, calling them to come to the surface.

A *bure*, or traditional village house — the frame is made from hardwood

And the giant turtles come to the surface to listen to this strange chant. Tradition has it that if anyone from the enemy village of Nabukelevu is present, the turtles will not come.

This part is not a myth—it really happens! Today, you can go to Namuana and listen to the maidens chanting their song and see the giant turtles lured to the surface of the bay.

Fiji has nearly three thousand different native plant species. As well as the common coconut palm, there is a wide range of hardwood trees and flowering bushes. The hardwood trees were used for canoe-building, or hollowed out to make the *lali,* or wooden gong. Each village has a *lali* in a prominent place. It is used to summon people to church, or for other formal occasions. These trees are also used to make the frames of *bures,* or houses.

Bamboo grows rampant in many places in Fiji and is often used in building. It is sometimes split and woven to make attractive and durable walls. Short bamboo poles are also used as a basic musical instrument. The Fijian musician, one pole in each hand, sets up a drum rhythm by banging on the ground. This beat is basic to many Fijian songs and dances.

Many colourful flowers are also native to Fiji. Among them is the rare tagimaucia—Fiji's national symbol. Hibiscus flowers are found in Fiji in a whole range of colours. An hibiscus flower

A dancer holding one of the short bamboo poles which Fijians use as a basic musical instrument

One of the many varieties of orchid which grow in Fiji

worn over the ear is a common decoration for both men and women. Many varieties of orchids also grow in Fiji. And there is a wide range of plants used as traditional medicines by the Fijians. Some appear to be highly effective. They are still used in addition to, or instead of, modern medicines.

And, of course, there are the tropical fruits always associated with the Pacific. Almost all tropical fruit can be grown in Fiji: bananas, pineapples, mangoes, oranges, breadfruit, mandarins, pawpaws—the list is endless.

Fijian root crops include those common to Polynesia—dalo, taro, yams and cassava—as well as the yaqona, the plant basic to Fijian culture.

31

Cannibals, Chiefs and Parliament

The history of Fiji is a story of immigration, of changes and of achievements. Fijian legend tells of a great chief named Lutunasobasoba who led his people across the seas to the new land of Viti. (This name was pronounced as *Fiji* by Europeans.) We know that the first people to live in Fiji were Melanesian tribesmen from South-East Asia. They came via the Indonesian islands. Since then, there have been other waves of migrating people: Micronesian, Polynesian and Papuan.

The first European to discover Fiji (in 1643) was a Dutchman named Abel Tasman. The English explorer James Cook came in 1774. But most of the early mapping and recording of Fiji was done by Captain William Bligh. He sailed there after the famous mutiny on the *Bounty* in 1789.

At this time, many of the Fijians were engaged in fierce tribal wars, and cannibalism was common. The Fijians were skilled and cunning fighters—many bloody battles were fought with spears and heavy clubs.

Most of the European visitors of this period were rough and tough too—whalers calling in to provision their ships, or traders coming to cut down the valuable sandalwood trees. These sailors were not above using their muskets to keep the native people at bay. Later, there were also "blackbirders". They indulged

An engraving of Captain James Cook, the English explorer who came to Fiji in 1774

in a notorious practice which was rife in the Pacific at that time. Sailing-ships would go to Pacific islands to "collect" men to work the cane-fields. The men would be enticed onto the ship, or simply captured, and then sold into a virtual slavery to plantation-owners.

Gradually, Europeans settled and established working relationships with the Fijians. Even in these times, the Europeans wrote of their politeness and refined customs. In 1844 the first missionary arrived. Although one or two were murdered, the missionaries spread through the islands, and their message was

A Catholic mission. Missionaries first arrived in Fiji in 1844

quickly received. By 1854, they had converted Fiji's most famous and paramount chief, Ratu Seru Cakobau.

This event marked the end of tribal wars and of cannibalism. More Europeans arrived, and trading-posts and plantations were established. The town of Levuka was the centre of the European community and, by this time, it was not uncommon to see fifty tall ships in its harbour. The United States civil war was causing a shortage of cotton in England, so cotton-planters were enjoying a boom period in Fiji. This prosperity was evidenced by the

34

fact that Levuka had over fifty drinking establishments—and no law enforcement.

In 1871, the European merchants and traders formed a governing body and proclaimed Chief Cakobau as King of Fiji. Not everyone was happy with this move—some plantation-owners refused to pay the taxes the new government tried to impose. At one stage it looked as if civil war would develop, with some planters barricading themselves into a hotel. But, with some persuasion resulting from the presence of a British naval vessel, and its threat of cannon-fire, the conflict was avoided.

However, the problem remained. Cakobau was not supported by enough of the plantation-owners to rule effectively. He was also under considerable pressure because of an inflated claim for damages from the Americans—as a result of the looting of the American Consul's house and the murder of an American citizen. The claim had risen to far more than the new government was able to pay.

Finally, Cakobau and the merchants asked Britain to take over the governing of the country. After Britain had twice refused, a Deed of Cession was signed in 1874, and Fiji became a British dependency. Almost one hundred years later, on October 10th, 1970, Fiji was granted independence, and became a member of the Commonwealth of Nations. During those ninety-six years Fiji had changed dramatically.

The most important change was the arrival of another wave of immigration. It was caused by the large sugar-cane plantations

Cutting sugar-cane today

which the Europeans had established. Labour was needed to
work the plantations, and the owners had hoped to employ the
Fijians. But the Fijians were not very interested. Then, in 1875,
there was an epidemic of measles. This was a new disease to
Fiji, and so its effects were very serious. Many of the islanders
died. The villages could barely grow enough food for themselves.
As a result, the government would not allow the plantation-
owners to employ people from the villages. Instead they brought

36

in workers from India. And, after their contracts ran out, many of the Indians stayed on. They became independent farmers and businessmen. Many of the big plantations were split up into small-holdings and leased to the Indians.

Today, fifty-five per cent of Fiji's population are of Indian descent. They are a bustling business-like people. It is they who own and control most of the shops, hotels and businesses. Fiji owes much of its wealth to their hard work. The Indians brought with them their culture and religion.

For nearly one hundred years Fiji was ruled by Governors General from Britain. The first of these, Sir Arthur Gordon, was a man of considerable foresight. He decided that the best way to rule Fiji was through the existing system of tribal chiefs. This may seem an obvious policy today, but in those days it was quite revolutionary, and was unique amongst the colonies. The more common attitude was to treat native populations as "savages" and to rule by force—a method which became known as "gunboat diplomacy".

So, in Fiji, the chiefs retained power, which meant the tribal system was perpetuated. This lead directly to continued communal ownership of land and to the second unique feature of the Fiji administration—the fact that only Fijians could own land in Fiji. Today, Fijians own eighty-two per cent of their country. Compare this to New Zealand, where the Maoris own ten per cent, or Hawaii, where the original inhabitants own virtually none of their own land. This rule has, however, caused some resentment amongst the Indian people in Fiji. Some Indian families have lived in Fiji for four generations, but they must lease the land to grow their crops from the indigenous Fijian. They feel that the colonial government favoured the Fijians too much.

This was the background against which an independent government was set up. A lot of the drive for independence had come from the Indians, who were determined to have a fairer

A modern Fijian "warrior"—his traditional appearance gives some indication of the fierce attitudes which led the early European settlers to describe his ancestors as "savages"

The government buildings in Suva

say in the governing of the country. The colonial government was anxious to preserve the place of the Fijian. The result was a system that allowed for both.

Not surprisingly, the parliamentary structure is similar to that of Britain. Fiji has what is known as a Westminster system. There are two "houses"—one elected and one appointed. Fiji pays homage to Queen Elizabeth II, who is also proclaimed Queen of Fiji. Her representative is the Governor General. He appoints the Upper House, called the Senate. There are twenty-two Senators who are nominated by the Great Council of Chiefs (they nominate eight), the Prime Minister (seven), the Leader of the Opposition (six) and a representative of Rotuma (one). The job of the Senate is to review legislation from the Lower

39

House. It also has the final say on matters concerning Fijian land. The Senate has a watchdog role, and can appoint committees of enquiry. The Lower House, called the House of Representatives, has fifty-two members elected from different electorates. The main aim of the electoral system is to make sure that all races share power. Citizens over twenty-one years of age must register on a National Roll, and on one of three separate Communal Rolls: Fijian, Indian or General. (The General Roll is for people who are neither Fijian or Indian.) When a citizen votes, he votes on his Communal Roll for a representative of his racial group, and he also votes on the National Roll for each of the three national representatives in his electorate.

In the House of Representatives, twenty-two members are Fijian, twenty-two are Indian and eight are ''other''. They are elected partly from the Communal Roll and partly from the National Roll. Most representatives belong to one of the political parties. The party with the most representatives elected, forms a government, which appoints a Prime Minister and other ministers. The party with the second greatest number forms the Opposition. Parties can combine to form a coalition if they wish.

This all sounds complicated, but it seems to work well. Fiji is renowned for its stable government, and all racial groups feel that they are fairly represented in the parliament. Elections for the House of Representatives are held every four years. The Senators are appointed for a six-year term.

The Queen of England, through her representative, has

A view of Suva, the Fijian capital, today

constitutional power. But the country is governed by the Senate, with the strong influence of the Tribal Chiefs, and by the House of Representatives, which is set up so that all races are fairly represented. The Government of Fiji is based in Suva, the capital city.

Cities, Rivers and Resorts

Viti Levu is the largest island in Fiji, covering 10,429 square kilometres, (4,026 square miles). On the south-east end is Suva, the capital of Fiji. Some 71,000 people live here. By world standards the town is small, but its inhabitants make up over ten per cent of Fiji's total population of 672,000.

Suva is the political and commercial centre of Fiji. The government and all the ministerial departments are located here. Banks, insurance companies and department stores, all have their head offices in Suva.

There is a good natural harbour, where cargo ships load the sugar, coconut-oil and many other products exported by Fiji. Suva is also a popular stop-over for cruise ships. The arrival of a passenger-liner is always a special occasion. Kings Wharf, at the bottom of town, fills with sightseers and street marketeers. In what is now a long-standing tradition, the Fiji Military Forces Band welcomes the ships at the dockside. Dressed in smart uniforms with *sulu* (woven cloth) skirts, they make a handsome sight as they march alongside the wharf. Their lively music is a joy both to the many local families who bring their children to hear it and to the tourists who line the decks of the ships.

Once they come ashore, the tourists face a sea of smiling faces—sword-sellers offering carved wooden swords, other

A handsome sight—the Fiji Military Forces Band

people selling shells, woven mats and handicrafts, and guides offering to show them where the ''best buys'' are. Although the atmosphere is bustling, there is a genuine warmth from the townspeople. Tourists rarely feel pressurized, but the natural charm of the Fijian can be very persuasive.

For the tourist the next stop is likely to be the municipal markets. These are busy at any time, but on the days when a passenger-liner is in port—called ''boat days''—they are filled to overflowing with market stalls. One side of the market is the major food supplier for Suva; it also provides an income for hundreds of people. The market sells fish, prawns, crab, eggplant and a whole range of tropical fruit and spices—food from all the different cultures of Fiji. The other side of the market is for handicrafts. Here visitors can choose from an amazing

43

An example of *masi*—Fijian cloth made from the inner bark of a tree

selection of wood carvings, *masi* (Fijian cloth), mats and baskets, shells and decorations of very high quality.

The keen bargain-hunter will probably go to the Cumming Street area next, since this is famous for its rows of duty-free shops. In order to promote tourism, in 1962, Fiji became "duty free"—no duty or sales tax is levied by the government on the sale of goods. Visitors can buy cameras, watches, radios and jewellery at prices far cheaper than in their home countries. The shops are staffed almost entirely by Indians and the atmosphere is very businesslike. Smartly dressed and very attentive young Indians stand behind each counter. Any sign of interest on the part of a customer will trigger off their sales talk. Most goods

44

Fijian wooden bowls. These and other local handicrafts are very popular with tourists who buy them as souvenirs

are marked with price tags higher than the price they will sell for; bargaining is very much part of the game. Tourists are advised to "shop around" to ensure that they get a good deal.

A stroll around the streets of Suva highlights how international the town is. A mixture of races and of architectural styles can be seen in all districts. There are Indians, Fijians, Chinese and Europeans—all dressed in their traditional styles. Many different languages are spoken. The buildings, too, form many contrasts. The parliament buildings are solid and English-looking. Old colonial hotels with verandahs around them stand alongside new

45

high-rise hotels with large swimming-pools. And the colonnade of Morris Hedstrom, Fiji's large department store, could have come straight out of Venice!

A visit to the Fiji Museum is a sudden reminder of the country's turbulent past. Weapons, tools and ornaments (from the days when Fiji was a land of warriors and cannibalism) are all on show. Carbon-dating of pottery pieces shows that Fiji was inhabited at least three thousand years ago.

The museum is also active as a research and educational institute. It organizes archaeological expeditions and lectures, and provides information on the language and culture of the Fijians. These are designed to make Fijian young people more aware of their cultural background.

Government buildings stand fortress-like on Victoria Parade. They are the repository of an interesting piece of Fiji's history. When Chief Cakobau signed the Deed of Cession in 1874, he presented his personal war-club to Queen Victoria, as a symbol of his acceptance of her rule. In 1932, King George V returned the club to Fiji and it became the mace of the Legislative Council. Today, it rests on the table in front of the Speaker. The head points to the side of the house where the party in power is seated, and the handle points to the Opposition.

In the centre of Albert Park is the Governor General's house. A lone sentry stands guard at the gate. A changing of the guard ceremony at advertised times attracts a large crowd of camera-clicking tourists. Elsewhere in Suva, in the suburbs, there are modern homes and also dilapidated old wooden houses. A white-

A Fiji Air plane unloading at Nausori. These planes fly regularly between the populated islands

domed Muslim mosque, Hindu temples and Christian churches all blend in amongst the guest-houses and apartment buildings.

And the rain. Many visitors' memories of Suva are of the sound of rain beating on corrugated iron. A tropical downpour is not just rain, it is buckets of water pouring down! You are totally drenched in seconds!

Suva's airport is 22 kilometres (nearly 14 miles) out of town, at Nausori, on the waterways of the Rewa Delta, which wind inland from Suva harbour. These waterways are the main means of transport to the inland villages. Water taxis—long canoe-like craft with outboard motors—can be seen arriving, loaded with passengers and goods. A trip along the delta takes passengers past fishing-boats, children swimming and bathing, and women doing the family washing on the banks. Everywhere, there are waving and smiling Fijians.

From Suva, Queens Road follows the southern coast of Viti Levu past tourist resorts and Fijian villages. The villages have no electricity; at night they are lit by kerosene lamps which hang in the houses and under the palm trees. The air is filled with the sounds of giggling children and laughing adults.

The resorts of this area—known as the Coral Coast—were some of the first established in Fiji. One of the more extensive is Pacific Harbour, just thirty minutes' journey from Suvu on a good highway. Here the tourist will find every facility required for a tropical holiday. There are shopping centres and sports complexes, and a reconstruction of a pre-European Fijian

Members of the National Dance Theatre of Fiji in their colourful traditional costume

village. Visitors can watch native girls beating *masi* (native cloth), weaving sennit (coconut fibres) into decorative panels and making pottery. There is also a *Bure Kalou* (temple) with its steeply pitched tower roof, where the spirit gods were believed to dwell. A strip of *masi* reaches from the roof to the floor. The high priest would sit at the base of this and go into a trance. The spirits would travel down the *masi* and speak through him. Offerings would be brought and the spirits would be consulted in this way before any major decisions were taken.

There is also a cultural centre here which features Fijian song and dance. The National Dance Theatre of Fiji perform here most nights. The traditional dances of Fiji have been carefully researched and they are executed with amazing vigour and vitality. Their drama and intensity overwhelms the audience. Through dance and mime the performers portray the legends of Fiji.

Further west along Queens Road is Sigatoka. It has a population of two thousand and it lies at the mouth of the Sigatoka River, known as the ''salad bowl'' of Fiji. On its fertile banks a wide variety of crops are grown—cabbage, cocoa, tapioca, tobacco, rice and many more. These provide the main source of income for the people of the surrounding area.

From Sigatoka, the road follows the coast to Nadi, the home of Fiji's International Airport. Nadi is the arrival point for most overseas tourists; it has many hotels and duty-free shops. An example of the effect of land being owned only by Fijian natives is found in one of the more expensive hotels. The owners have had to lease the land from the nearby villagers and, as part of the deal, the villagers get first option on the available jobs in the hotel.

Nadi is the most important sugar-cane growing area in Fiji. The land is flat, dry and fertile, with a good water supply from the rivers.

Just north of Nadi is Lautoka, a port town that serves the islands to the west of Viti Levu. Lautoka is Fiji's second largest city, with 26,000 people. From here ferries take visitors to the resort islands—Castaway Island, Treasure Island, Beachcomber Island—each catering to a different tourist taste, but all "selling" sunshine, and Fijian hospitality and charm.

Cargo-ships and island traders bring copra, fish and vegetables from the villages on the larger islands to Lautoka.

Duty-free shops in Nadi, the arrival point for most visitors to Fiji coming by air, many of whom also stay in Nadi's hotels

Castaway Island seen from the sea. This is a typical tourist resort being developed to provide a full range of amenities

They return with kerosene, cement, flour and canned milk.

The famous Blue Lagoon cruise ships are also based in Lautoka. Thousands of passengers each year enjoy round-trips to the offshore islands.

From Lautoka, travellers go north along the coast, on Kings Road. Rows of mango trees, planted by early settlers, line the roadside. To the north is the quiet town of Ba, with a population of seven thousand.

From there, the road passes several smaller villages and resorts. The hills inland from there contain Fiji's gold-mines. Turning inland along the Wainibuka River, the scenery changes—for the first time there are no palm trees. This is dairy and beef cattle country—flat plains and grassy fields. Behind

51

The interior of the small church which has become famous for the painting *The Black Christ*

them, rise tiers of mountain ranges, fading into purple and mauves.

Just off the main road is Nanukuloa. Here, in a small church, is a mural by the internationally famous painter, Jean Charlot. In a space behind the altar, about ten metres (32 feet) wide by three metres (nearly ten feet) high, is the painting known as *The Black Christ*. It shows a dark-skinned Christ on the cross, wearing a *masi sulu*. The painting is also full of symbolic references to the races of Fiji—there are boys offering gifts of *masi* and *tabua* (whale's tooth); a majestic Indian lady carrying a garland of flowers; missionaries; working oxen; and war clubs. The painting was completed in 1963 at the request of the chaplain, a close friend of Jean Charlot. So here, in this remote corner of Fiji, in a small country church, we find an internationally recognized work of art!

Following the river, the vegetation becomes more lush as we come to the wet side of Viti Levu, and then on to Suva where our journey began. The round trip is about 500 kilometres (310 miles).

The interior of Viti Levu is sparsely populated. The land is mountainous and largely covered in rain forest on the south-east side, and in dryer bush on the north-western side. There is no regular transport, and there are few roads. Some of the more accessible parts have pine plantations, but the majority remains in its natural state.

Plantations, Legends and Firewalkers

Fiji's second largest island, Vanua Levu, covers 5,556 square kilometres (over 2,000 square miles). Few tourists get to Vanua Levu. There are some hotels, but few duty-free shops or craft markets. There are extensive plantations, many privately owned, in very beautiful settings. Huge bushes of tropical flowers grow here; and ferns and orchids, as well as coconut and banana trees, cascade right to the edge of the sandy beaches.

On the dryer northern side of the island there are some sugar and rice plantations, but Vanua Levu, like most of the smaller islands, still relies largely on copra for its income. There are two towns, Savusavu (with 2,600 people) and Labasa (with 5,000 people). Labasa is inland on a tidal river. It is the agricultural centre of the island.

The overwhelming impression of Vanua Levu is of lush growth. Yet the title of "Garden Island of Fiji" is given to Taveuni, an island of 470 square kilometres (182 square miles) off the east coast of Vanua Levu. Taveuni has the highest rainfall in all Fiji, resulting in a thick green tropical growth.

There are extensive coconut plantations here too, mostly privately owned by Europeans. The centre of the island is a high volcanic mountain with a lake in its crater. On the shores of this lake (and nowhere else in the world) grows the spectacularly

A scene at Labasa market — at the heart of the agricultural area of the island

beautiful red and white tagimaucia flower—the national symbol of Fiji. One of these flowers was presented to Queen Elizabeth during her last visit to Fiji.

South from Taveuni, quite close to Viti Levu is the island of Ovalau. It has an area of 101 square kilometres (39 square miles), most of which is rugged and heavily wooded. The biggest town, Levuka, now old and sleepy, was once the centre of activity in Fiji. Levuka was the first capital where the trading-ships came and the government was established. Here, too, is where the Deed of Cession was signed.

By 1870, the export of cotton was booming, and new business houses crowded the one narrow street. As the street was backed by high hills there was nowhere to expand. Crime and violence became rife, with large amounts of spirits being sold and consumed.

In 1881, the decision was made to move the capital to Suva. And, as if finally to end the town's boom era, in 1888 a hurricane destroyed many of the buildings which had links with the colourful past. Today they have a saying in Levuka: ''When God made time, he made plenty of it''. The locals are content to live their life at a relaxed pace, and to let the world go by.

Levuka is the home of Fiji's oldest school; it was established in 1879. It is also where Fiji's first newspaper—the *Fiji Times* —started in 1869. It is flourishing still in the new capital of Suva.

All the copra from the surrounding area was once exported through Levuka, and this provided an income for many of the townspeople. But with the change in world markets, Fiji now processes the copra into coconut oil. The processing plant was built in Suva, and so Levuka lost its shipping trade.

Today, a fishing industry has been established, employing many locals in the processing and canning of tuna. The industry is government-owned, but contracts vessels from New Zealand, Taiwan, Japan, Korea and Tonga to catch the fish. Canned fish earns nearly ten per cent of Fiji's export income.

56

Yet, in the streets of Levuka, the overwhelming impression is of a quiet town reflecting on its past glories. This atmosphere has a charm of its own, and is a nice contrast to the busy progressive cities of the main island.

Far out to the west is a group of tiny islands known as Lau. These islands have a special charm to Fijians, and an important place in their history. They are renowned for their magical beauty. The southernmost islands in the group are closer to Tonga than to Fiji's main island. The group has been an important meeting-place for the people of both lands throughout their histories. Lau was once controlled by Tongan chiefs and,

A Taiwanese fishing-boat unloading at Levuka

An aerial view of the tiny island of Bau, off the coast of Viti Levu

even today, the people of Lau are more Polynesian—and lighter-skinned—than the main islanders.

Lau is also the homeland of the Prime Minister of Fiji, Ratu Sir Kamisese Mara, G.C.K.G., K.B.E.

There is no guest accommodation in Lau. Visitors must stay with relatives or friends, and traditional Fijian customs are expected to be followed, before and during their stay.

Close inshore to Viti Levu is the tiny island of Bau. At low tide it is possible to walk to it across a coral causeway. Bau is just 1.5 kilometres (less than one mile) long, and only 15 metres (49 feet) above sea level at its highest point. It has always been the home of the Paramount Chief of Fiji. From this tiny island Chief Cakobau ruled Fiji. The dialect of Bau is the standard

58

for Fijian dialects. Traditionally, to visit Bau gave a person status. Today, the population is just 300—many fewer than the 4,000 of one hundred years ago. However, the island is still the home of the highest chiefs and it has a special place in Fijian culture.

Off the southern coast of Viti Levu is the island of Beqa. Beqa is a volcanic island with a very extensive coral reef and lagoon. It has a steep rocky interior, with nine villages dotted around its coastline. The villagers, almost entirely native Fijians, live a communal life. Much of their working time is spent working for the community, but increasingly there is pressure to work on private schemes.

Education is causing the young people in the islands to reject their inherited status, and to seek equal opportunity. Young people with higher education tend to leave for paid jobs in the cities. This breaking down of the traditional system is a general problem in village life throughout Fiji.

Another change is apparent in the construction of their houses. With timber and thatching materials becoming more difficult to find, it can take many weeks for a small team to collect all the necessary materials to build a house, called a *bure*. The construction may also take weeks. With the breaking down of the communal systems, a villager may have to pay towards the cost of this labour. So it is cheaper to build a house of concrete blocks with a corrugated iron roof. Thatched *bures* require almost constant maintenance, and usually have a life of around ten years. The concrete houses require no maintenance, and will last much longer. As a result almost all new *bures* are of concrete. Within a few decades, there may be very few traditional *bures* left.

Fishing in their extensive lagoon has been a source of income for Beqans for a long time, but recently they have replaced this with performances at tourist hotels. For the people of Beqa have the ability to walk on fire! Beqa is known as the "Island of Fire-walkers".

The members of the Sawau tribe are able to walk on white hot stones. They perform this feat regularly at tourist hotels in Fiji. An elaborate preparation ceremony is carried out under supervision of the *Bete* (high priest). The men segregate themselves for two weeks before the event, and have no contact whatsoever with women. They also must not eat any coconut. On the day a large pit is dug and lined with river stones. A huge log fire is built over them some six to eight hours before the ceremony. The *Bete* collects dry tree ferns which he uses to make anklets for the firewalkers. When the time comes the village men clear the burning logs, chanting *O-Vulo-Vulo*. When the *Bete* is satisfied, he jumps onto the rocks to test their firmness. He then calls *Vuto-O* and the firewalkers come at a brisk trot and walk onto the stones, gathering in the centre and chanting. Their tinder dry anklets do not ignite.

After the ceremony, the anklets are buried, along with baskets of special roots, in the pit. Four days later they are uncovered, the baked roots are ground up and mixed with water. This water is used to cook *taro* which is eaten by the firewalkers.

The firewalkers show no sign of pain during the performance,

60

A man digging taro—this is the root crop eaten by the firewalkers

and their feet are unharmed by the ordeal. Scientists have not been able to explain how this is possible.

Firewalking used to be performed on special occasions only, but now it has become more commercialized. It is a very impressive ceremony to watch. Doubting spectators are often invited to approach the pit, and find they are unable even to get close to it because of the heat. This is enough to convince even the most sceptical!

South of Beqa is the island of Kadavu. It is a volcanic island,

Firewalkers walking on white-hot stones by the lakeside

with an area of 411 square kilometres (159 square miles). Kadavu has many very beautiful harbours and bays. Although it is at present off the tourist track, it has a growing reputation as a diving location. The villagers of Kadavu swim and fish with no fear of attack from sharks. They believe they are protected by Dakuwaqa, the Shark God. When local fishermen go out for a night's fishing they reverently pour a bowl of *yaqona* into the sea for Dakuwaqa.

To the west of Viti Levu lies the Yasawa group. There are twenty islands of volcanic origin in the group. They have become well-known because of the regular three-day "Blue Lagoon" cruises which take tourists to their villages and bays. About five thousand people, almost entirely Fijian, live in the Yasawas. Copra is a major source of income but, for the villages where the tourist boats stop, this is supplemented by markets set up on the beaches, selling shell necklaces, *masi* and handicrafts. The tourists are brought ashore in small boats. Local custom requires that they visit the church first. They can then wander around the village or inspect the markets. Eager Fijian adults and children sit cross-legged on mats, with their craftwork spread out in front of them.

There is one more notable island. It is Rotuma, 390 kilometres (240 miles) north of Viti Levu. Although Rotuma is administered by Fiji, its people are of a different ethnic origin from the Fijians. The Rotumans are Polynesians, more like the Hawaiians and Maoris.

Rotuma was once a favourite resort for escaped convicts and runaway sailors, and it has a lively history of European contact. The Rotumans appoint one member to the Senate of Fiji. Of the population of 8,300, about 4,100 live on the island, the rest having migrated to Viti Levu, where they have unrestricted access and right to work permits.

The island has a good road around its coast, a total distance

A Fijian woman weaving a mat. Weaving is a traditional skill which attracts many tourists, as well as producing useful articles

of 27 kilometres (16 miles), and a number of cars and trucks operate there. The land is very fertile, and almost any tropical fruit or vegetable can be grown. Rotumans were always known for their ability as canoe-builders and navigators. They had wandered the Pacific before the Europeans arrived. Today, they are known for their fine woven mats, which are much in demand. An island trading-ship calls every four months at Rotuma to collect copra but, like most offshore islands, the airstrip is Rotuma's link with the outside world.

Family, Food and Sports

The Fijians are well-known for their friendliness. Their greeting of *Bula* (Hello) is usually given with a warm genuine smile. They enjoy life at a slower pace than the Indians or Europeans, and are relaxed and easy-going. They believe life is to be lived and enjoyed now, and they enjoy talking, singing and the company of others.

By comparison, the Indian is a much busier person. The Indians enjoy work and success, and value these highly. They have also retained their religion and culture. Indian women wear saris and have the traditional coloured caste mark on their foreheads.

Most Indians are followers of Hindu, Muslim or Sikh beliefs. The temples of these religions are found in all Fijian cities, and their festivals are celebrated regularly. For example, in October Hindus celebrate the Festival of Diwali (called the Festival of Lights). When darkness comes, hundreds of tiny lamps and candles are lit, to fill every dark corner with light, and fireworks also light the sky. The festival celebrates the triumph of good over evil. Because it is a time of enjoyment and fun, people of all religions and races join in. It becomes a time for general celebration and children especially look forward to it each year.

An Indian woman—easily recognized by her sari and traditional caste mark—returning from the fish market

The Fijians are mostly Christians, as a result of the groundwork done by the early missionaries. The Methodist and Catholic religions are predominant but the newer American-based Christian sects are gaining in popularity.

Fijians who live in the few remaining traditional villages have strong ties with their *matagali,* or sub-tribe. Traditionally, when

67

they marry, women live with their husband's family. So the *matagali* follows the male line of descent. Seniority is also important. A younger brother is expected to obey and respect his older brother who, in turn, must protect and care for him. The most senior member of the family is always served first at meal-times. Family elders are not expected to work, but their presence at a workplace gives a task added importance or status.

Fijians also have strong ties with their families. These ties extend through the *matagali*. For example, a Fijian regards his brothers' children as his own. They may even call him ''Father''. Relatives work together to support the whole family. Everyone will take responsibility for the misconduct of any one member.

To a Fijian, a *vanua,* or homeland, is much more than just the land; it also covers the people, customs and beliefs of that area. For a Fijian, the *vanua* is where his roots are. It is a place he identifies with and feels confident in. It is also the place he will choose to be taken back to when he dies.

Another major feature of Fijian culture is the tradition of reciprocation—the giving and receiving of gifts. This is very important in Fijian social life, and there are complex rules which decide what and how much is given. A casual visit between friends may call for a gift of food, with hospitality being shown in return. The gifts will show the social status of both parties, so great care is taken not to embarrass the receiver or to appear ungenerous. Reciprocation is usually something that goes on over a long period of time, with each trying to out-do the other.

Gift-giving is an important part of transactions such as obtaining the use of a piece of land, or getting help to build a house or plant crops, or even getting approval for a marriage. The acceptance of gifts often means the acceptance of an obligation, and to refuse would be insulting. The gifts are often worth a great amount of money, but it is always the giving and acceptance which is important.

All traditional village ceremonies involve food and drink. Fiji's national drink is *yaqona* or *kava*, made from the *yaqona* plant, which is a type of pepper. The roots of the plant are dried, then ground up and placed in a *tanoa*—a bowl carved from wood. Water is added and the mixture is stirred until it is clear. The mixing of *yaqona* is an important part of all ceremonies, and strict rituals are followed. *Yaqona* is drunk from a *bilo*—a polished half coconut shell. It is also a drink for social occasions, where the formal rituals do not have to be followed.

Whenever a group of Fijians are sitting around enjoying themselves, a *tanoa* will be found. The *bilo* is handed round in turn to everyone in the group, and visitors or passing friends will generally be invited to join in.

Presentation of *magiti* (food) also plays a major part in all ceremonies. This may be cooked in a *lovo* (earth oven). Meat, vegetables and fish are wrapped in leaves and placed in an earth pit already filled with hot stones. The pit is then covered with coconut palm-fronds, banana leaves and earth and left to cook for several hours. The food comes out beautifully tender and

Musicians with a *tanoa* containing *kava*, the drink made from *yaqona*

with a distinctive flavour. A *lovo* is generally used when a large number of people will be sharing the food, such as during a village feast.

Of the many traditional Fijian gifts, there are two which have a special meaning. The first is the *tabua,* or whale's tooth. Each tooth is stained, oiled and polished, then fitted with a cord of local fibres. It is a great honour to be presented with a *tabua*. They are given to important guests, to mark a special occasion such as a wedding, or to resolve a dispute.

A villager returning home after a long time away may need many *tabuas* to present on his arrival. The *tabua* is such an important Fijian custom that the government has forbidden its export, except with a special permit.

The other important gift is *masi,* a cloth made from the inner bark of a tree. The bark is laid over a rounded log and beaten with wooden paddles to a fine texture. It starts off quite thick and about fifteen centimetres (six inches) wide. After beating, it thins out to a width of about fifty centimetres (twenty inches). Strips are fused together by overlapping and beating, and in this way a cloth of any size can be made. It is decorated with natural dyes using stencils cut from banana leaves. The colours vary from dull red to orange and brown. The patterns vary from district to district. *Masi* is the traditional cloth of the Fijian—it is used for ceremonial clothes, and as a decoration in homes. On special occasions many *masi* may be presented. The art of *masi*-making was almost lost with the arrival in Fiji of European fabrics, but now hand-craft co-operatives have been set up in the villages, and *masi* is sold to tourists. This has also revived its use by the villagers.

During the day, the rhythm of the paddles beating is a constant background to the laughter and other sounds of village life. It is a sound the old people associate with a village and enjoy hearing again.

The traditional Fijian home is called a *bure.* The foundation is generally a raised earth mound. This mound, or site, belongs to the first occupant and his male descendants. No one else can use it without permission—it is a sacred possession of the family. A *bure* frame is made from wooden posts tied together. Reeds or leaves are used to make a thatched roof and walls. There are no partitions inside, but different areas have special importance. For example, the back of the *bure* is considered private—for the family only—and visitors should not go there. Next to that is a less private part where honoured guests are allowed. The front has a fireplace, and is used for cooking and dishwashing; it is the public part of the *bure.*

There is almost no furniture—Fijians sit and sleep on mats on the ground. Fires are usually kept burning to keep mosquitoes away, and to keep the thatch hard. The fire is also a symbol of life, and shows that the household is well cared for.

Traditionally, Fijians light a fire by rubbing a stick very rapidly up and down a groove in a piece of wood. When the stick smoulders they add dry leaves and blow gently on it. This is quite a laborious method. Once started, cooking-fires are kept burning slowly when not in use.

The Fijians' native foods include root crops, such as yams, dalo and cassava; tree fruits, such as coconuts and bananas; meat—especially wild pork, and fish. They are skilled reef fishermen. Armed only with a long thin spear they walk amongst the shallows in the lagoons, and spear fish with great accuracy. They also use nets, boats and a wide variety of fish-traps to collect their seafood.

Within a village the traditional social status of a person is sharply defined. The son of a chief will always come before the son of a worker; an elder brother before his younger brother. And the roles of sons and daughters are very different. This inherited status has nothing to do with an individual's ability, and it is this part of village life which is under pressure today.

A man pulling cassava (tapioca) — one of Fiji's staple root crops

Beef cattle grazing. The Fijian diet includes meat—traditionally wild pork but also beef

Education, in particular, puts pressure on this system. The young people today feel that a person who has academic qualifications should rank before one who has none, regardless of their inherited position.

Traditionally, the chief of a village ruled the lives of its villagers. Most of the work they did was under his direction, and for the benefit of the whole community. Today there is more pressure for time off to work on private enterprise schemes.

Despite these pressures, the amount of communal sharing in a Fijian village far exceeds that usually found in a European society. In a Fijian village, if you go on a journey it is considered shameful to lock your house, in case friends or relatives wish to use it. If you have visitors, it is common to find baskets of food left on your doorstep, to help with feeding the extra people. In this way, assistance is given with no acknowledgement being sought or required.

Villagers also accept responsibility for all the children of the village. A young man may leave the village to live and work in the city. If he marries and has children he will at some time make a pilgrimage back to his village and present his children to it. It will be taken for granted that, if he dies, the village will adopt and support these children.

The overwhelming impression of village life is still the Fijians' friendliness and laughter. As they go about their work, and move from one celebration to the next, visitors cannot help but be impressed with their ability to enjoy life minute by minute. Their unhurried, untroubled ways, sometimes so frustrating to people from other cultures, win everyone over in the end.

Fijians enjoy teamwork and social contact, so sporting events are very popular. The islanders have all the basic ingredients needed to make good sportsmen. They are physically well-built, used to accepting the discipline of a leader, and born into a sharing and helping lifestyle. Not surprisingly, they enjoy games like Rugby and soccer—the two most popular sports in Fiji. From school level, teams are formed: village against village, district against district. It is Rugby on Saturday and football on Sunday.

A man holding coconut husks. His physique is an example of why the Fijians are such powerful sportsmen

Except at a national level, new spectators could be forgiven for thinking some of the standards are appalling. This would be because they have not grasped the basic principle: that the game is more important than winning! In Fiji you ask ''Did you enjoy it?'' rather than ''Did you win?''

Rugby and football are the main spectator sports, but many other games are enjoyed too—basketball, volleyball, netball, squash, tennis and hockey—and, of course, athletics are enjoyed at all levels.

War Canoes, Jet Planes and Sugar

The early Fijians were great canoe-builders. The *drua*—double canoe—was a most impressive sight. The hulls were made from planks of timber hewn from the forest, and lashed together with sennit (braided cords). Each hull was over thirty metres (98 feet) in length. A tall mast held a large woven sail. Several men were needed to handle the huge steering-oar. Three hundred men could be transported across oceans in this way with amazing speed. The mast could be swung round, steering the canoe in the opposite direction, and making it very easy to manoeuvre. Many early European explorers wrote accounts of the *drua*. A naval commodore wrote in 1841, "It had a magnificent appearance with its immense sail of white mats, the pennants streaming from the yards—its velocity was almost inconceivable." Before Christianity came to Fiji, *druas* were usually launched using the bodies of captured enemies as rollers—a practice which horrified the Europeans. *Druas* were war-canoes, but Fijians also made smaller double-hulled sailing-craft for fishing and transport. Few of these survive today, but they were once a common sight around the coastline. Dugout canoes, made from single logs and paddled, are still quite common in rivers and sheltered waters.

Today, the villagers use regular ferries for transport to main

Boys paddling a dugout canoe made from a single log

centres. Wooden boats, between four and ten metres (thirteen and thirty-two feet) in length, are used for fishing and transport between islands. They are generally powered by outboard motors.

On land, most islands with sufficient population have a bus service. In remote areas this may be fairly infrequent, or simply be a community-owned van which transports people and goods for a fixed fare. Many a joke has been made about the buses in some parts of Fiji being "air conditioned"—they simply have no windows! This is a pleasant and practical way to travel in such a good climate—blinds are pulled down over the openings if it rains.

But it is air travel that has opened up Fiji to the businessman and the tourist. Almost every populated island that is large enough has a grass airstrip. The very small islands are served by seaplanes. The air service is also the islanders' link with hospitals.

The colourful Fiji Air aircraft operate scheduled flights between the main centres of Viti Levu, and between Suva and the other populated islands of the Fiji Group. Fiji also boasts an international airline—Air Pacific. They operate large aircraft between Nadi, their base, and most other Pacific islands. They also have flights to Australia and New Zealand. Air Pacific plays an important role in Fiji's tourist development.

There are several other companies, with names like Sunflower Airlines and Turtle Airways. These operate scheduled flights, and are available for charter and sightseeing trips.

Private cars and trucks are the most common method of transport within Viti Levu. Taxis and rental cars are common in all the main centres. Fiji has no passenger-train service, but a single-track narrow-gauge railway is used to transport sugar-cane to the processing plants.

Sugar-cane is Fiji's biggest export product. And it was the sugar-cane which first brought the Indians to Fiji. Today, most of the cane is grown on small-holdings by Indians. The sugar is crushed and refined by the government-owned Fiji Sugar Corporation. Planting and cutting cane is all done by hand, and it involves a lot of hard work. Small railway trains are used to gather the cane. The tracks are moved around, often by bullocks, to reach all parts of the plantation.

Sugar earns over half of Fiji's export income—over half a

million tonnes a year is sold to the European Economic Community. Some twenty thousand small farms together employ about one quarter of Fiji's workforce. The amount Fiji earns from sugar depends on the world price and on the volume produced. In 1970, there was a major price slump. This caused a lot of unemployment in rural areas, and had a serious effect on Fiji's economy. The price has since recovered but, in 1983, a hurricane caused extensive damage to the crop, greatly reducing Fiji's earnings in that year.

For these reasons the government is trying to reduce the economy's dependence on sugar, by encouraging new industries. The most important of these is tourism. Fiji is said to be the hub of the South Pacific—a logical stop-over for tourists crossing the Pacific. In fact, when Charles Kingsford-Smith made the first aircraft flight from America to Australia in 1928, he made a stop-over in Fiji—landing in Suva's central park!

One of the small trains used on single-track lines to transport sugar-cane

The Fiji Visitors Bureau—tourism is an important source of income in the islands

Many people in Fiji see tourism as important to their future. It brings trade and wealth to their communities. And Fijians have a genuine enjoyment of visitors. The government is actively encouraging overseas investment in tourism, and some very large land development schemes have been started within the last few years.

82

Fiji has a lot to offer to the tourist—a good climate, natural beauty, modern facilities and, most of all, the very friendly people. It is not surprising that the tourist industry is growing rapidly.

Fiji's forest industry, sometimes called its "green gold", is the subject of much research and development. Large areas have been planted with pine trees, especially on land not suitable for

A girl sorting pine seedlings—it will take some time before this "green gold" will mature

A sawmill near Korovou on Viti Levu

crops. It will be some years before Fiji will reap the benefits of these, but high hopes are held for the future. Native hardwoods are milled from the huge natural rain forest. There is a re-afforestation programme to ensure this resource is not depleted. Coconut oil made from copra is also important, as it is a major source of income for many villages, especially in the more isolated areas.

Other significant export industries are canned fish from the processing plant in Levuka, and gold from the mines in Viti Levu.

Fiji currently has a trade gap—that is the islanders spend more on importing than they earn on exporting. To reduce this gap the government is not only encouraging the exporting industries, it is also promoting "import substitution" industries—those which make goods which would otherwise be imported. These goods include meat, clothing, footware and manufactured goods.

There is also a full range of service industries, such as printing, engineering, advertising, data processing, real estate, travel and finance institutions.

Nearly a quarter of Fiji's import budget is spent on petroleum products, mostly from Australia. Fiji has no oil production of its own. Other major imports are food items from New Zealand and Australia, and machinery from Japan, Australia and the United Kingdom.

Schools, Forums and Achievements

The best way for any country to invest in its future is in the health and education of its people. This Fiji has done, and this policy is already showing results. Fiji is a healthy country, free from most tropical diseases. Infant mortality in Fiji is amongst the lowest in the world. Water supplies are modern and carefully supervised—the tap water is drinkable in all areas. Health clinics have been set up throughout Fiji to care for the people.

Fiji's Medical School was started by the colonial government, in 1887. They trained native medical practitioners, not only for Fiji, but for other Pacific islands too. During those early years, when transport and communications were poor, the British doctors could not have coped alone. But, through the school, a local person from each area was trained, and he then returned to his people with his skills. Fiji's good health today owes much to the N.M.P. Scheme.

Education in Fiji has seen great improvements in the last twenty years. At present thirty-two per cent of Fiji's national budget is spent on education. Now primary schools are available free of charge for every child between six and ten. Although education is not compulsory, over ninety-eight per cent of children of this age attend. Primary schools are almost all mono-racial. This has occurred because of the language difference,

86

Children like these can now expect education and health care to be readily available in Fiji

Schoolchildren in the school grounds

and because of the system of operating schools by committee. Where a community feel there is a need for a primary school, they form a committee to establish and run the school. They then apply to the government and, if they qualify, they are given the necessary funds and teachers. Naturally, the Indians and Fijians have each formed committees in their own communities, and so established their own schools.

There are 660 primary schools, and 140 secondary schools (for ages 11 to 16). Fees are payable at secondary school. If a family cannot afford the fees the government will pay in part or in full. This ensures equal opportunity for all children. Fiji has achieved a teacher/pupil ratio of 1:30—an impressive level in such a short space of time.

Fiji also has a university—the University of the South Pacific. This was established in 1968 in co-operation with other South Pacific islands. Today, there are students from Fiji and from many of the smaller island states.

There are also thirty-seven technical or vocational schools in Fiji. These cover a wide range of skills, including seamanship, hotel services, catering, mechanical engineering and horticulture.

Fiji today plays a role in international affairs and has a seat as an independent member of the United Nations.

Fiji is also active in the South Pacific Forum, an organization set up to provide some of the services previously provided by the colonial governments. By joining together, the many small island states of the Pacific have been able to have a stronger voice in international affairs, and to help each other with economic and political problems. This has led to a network of co-operation being set up.

Now, over two hundred organizations have been formed. These cover training institutions, church organizations, labour unions, news and information services and many more. This has greatly strengthened Fiji's ability to organize and develop its economy, and to develop its human resources.

The next few decades could see Fiji's investment in tourism and forestry bringing a major boost to the economy. There is

89

A yacht at anchor—sailing in these calm waters is a major tourist attraction in Fiji

Sunfish—one of the many varieties of fish which are caught off the coasts of Fiji. The Fijians are (and always have been) skilled fishermen

also another major resource which is as yet untapped. Along with the other countries in the South Pacific Forum, Fiji has declared a special Economic Zone. That is, Fiji has control of all the resources within 320 kilometres (200 miles) of its coastline. Because the Fiji islands are so spread out, this zone covers a massive one million square kilometres (386,000 square miles) of ocean. In the short term, this means a high fish resource but, in the long term, it may mean valuable minerals and oil from the sea-bed.

Fiji today has an economy which is growing and strengthening. The government is committed to a policy of steady growth towards economic independence, and it is committed to training the local people to do this. Unemployment is estimated at seven per cent, but there is a great shortage of skilled people. There are few Europeans working in Fiji, and some people feel the islanders should employ more experts from overseas to speed up the development programme. However, the policy of the government is that local people must learn these skills, and this learning is an important part of the development programme.

Fiji has a strong heritage—a lifestyle rare in today's world. The Fijians are a friendly, sharing, seemingly carefree people. Tourism will inevitably bring western civilization and values, and some people fear that this will have a negative influence on the Fijians. Yet the more optimistic believe that the Fijians will remain unique as a people.

So, as Fiji moves forward, we see a country with a firm hold on its national heritage, a government which fairly represents its people, a nation renowned for its stability, and for its economy which has a steady and controlled growth rate: a list of achievements most countries would envy!

Index

95